W9-CTC-272

Deer

Leo Statts

abdopublishing.com

Published by Abdo Zoom™, PO Box 398166, Minneapolis, Minnesota 55439. Copyright © 2018 by Abdo Consulting Group, Inc. International copyrights reserved in all countries. No part of this book may be reproduced in any form without written permission from the publisher. Abdo Zoom™ is a trademark and logo of Abdo Consulting Group, Inc.

Printed in the United States of America, North Mankato, Minnesota
042017
092017

Cover Photo: Shutterstock Images
Interior Photos: Eric Isselee/Shutterstock Images, 1; Janusz Pienkowski/Shutterstock Images, 4–5; Dave M. Hunt Photography/iStockphoto, 5; iStockphoto, 6, 7, 8–9, 10, 14, 15, 17, 18–19; Red Line Editorial, 9, 20 (left), 20 (right), 21 (left), 21 (right); Sue Smith/iStockphoto, 11; Rodrigo Bellizzi/iStockphoto, 12–13; Frank Hildebrand/iStockphoto, 16

Editor: Brienna Rossiter
Series Designer: Madeline Berger
Art Direction: Dorothy Toth

Publishers Cataloging-in-Publication Data
Names: Statts, Leo, author.
Title: Deer / by Leo Statts.
Description: Minneapolis, MN : Abdo Zoom, 2018. | Series: Backyard animals | Includes bibliographical references and index.
Identifiers: LCCN 2017931124 | ISBN 9781532120039 (lib. bdg.) | ISBN 9781614797142 (ebook) | ISBN 9781614797708 (Read-to-me ebook)
Subjects: LCSH: Deer--Juvenile literature. | Animals--Juvenile literature.
Classification: DDC 599.65--dc23
LC record available at http://lccn.loc.gov/2017931124

Table of Contents

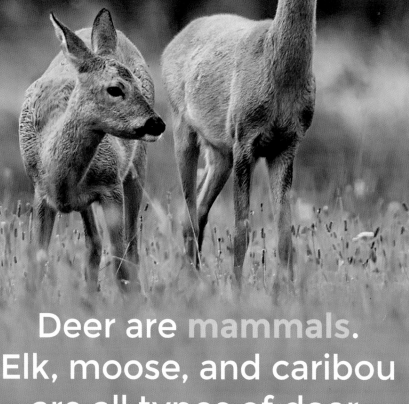

Deer

Deer are **mammals.**
Elk, moose, and caribou
are all types of deer.

Male deer are
called bucks. They are
known for their antlers.

Deer can be many sizes.
A deer's fur can be
brown or gray.

Some deer
have white spots
on their fur.

Habitat

White-tailed deer are common in North America. But deer can be found all around the world. They often live in places with lots of trees.

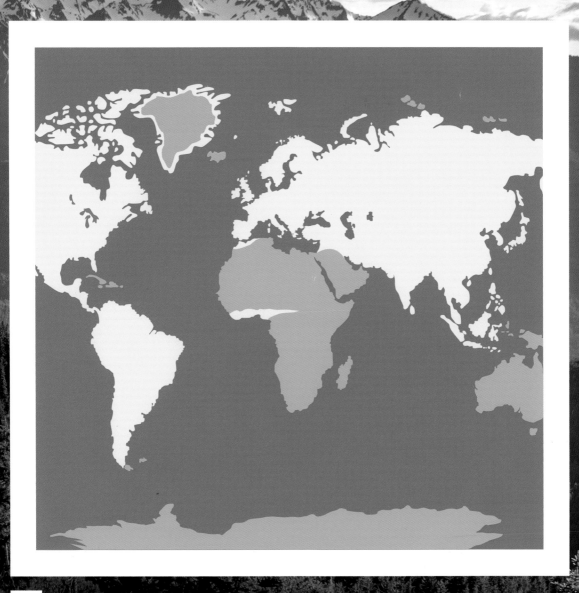

Where deer live

Deer also live near mountains or fields.

Some deer even live in cities.

Food

Deer eat plants.
They mostly eat grass and leaves.

They also eat tree bark. Sometimes deer eat fruits and vegetables, too.

Deer are ruminants.

They swallow their food.
Then they bring the food
back up to chew it again.

A **doe** has one to three **fawns** at a time.

Fawns leave their mothers after one or two years.

Some types of deer live alone.
Others live in groups called herds.

Deer can live up to
15 years in the wild.

Quick Stats

Average Weight – Lightest

A Northern pudu weighs less than a bowling ball.

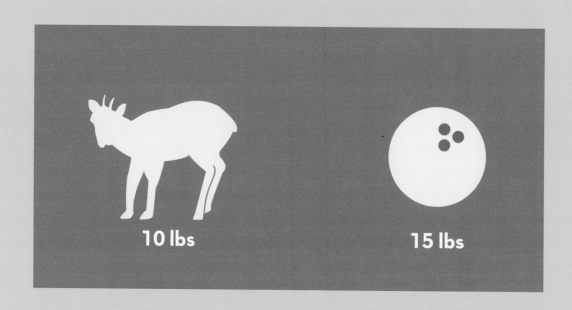

10 lbs   15 lbs

Average Weight – Heaviest

A moose weighs less than a soda vending machine.

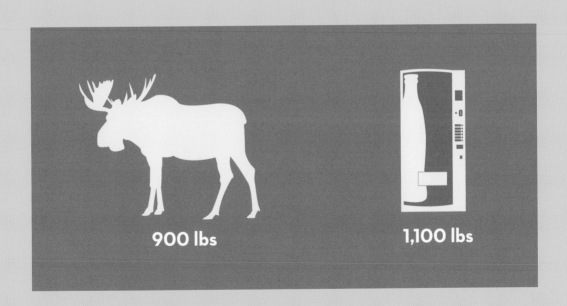

900 lbs   1,100 lbs

Glossary

antlers - bones that grow from a deer's head.

buck - a male deer.

doe - a female deer.

fawn - a young deer.

mammal - an animal that makes milk to feed its young and usually has hair or fur.

ruminant - an animal that has more than one stomach and chews cud.

Booklinks

For more information on deer, please visit abdobooklinks.com

Zoom In on Animals!

Learn even more with the Abdo Zoom Animals database. Check out abdozoom.com for more information.

Index